MW00873854

IT'S OFFICIAL!
YOU HAVE PROBLEMS!

BUT DON'T WORRY NOW YOU HAVE AN OUTLET FOR YOUR ANGER

INSIDE THIS BOOK YOU WILL FIND 20 MANDALAS FOR YOU TO SIT BACK AND COLOR

EACH ONE CONTAINS A PROBLEM THAT YOU SHOULD DEFINITELY BE ABLE TO RELATE TO!

HAPPY COLORING

COLORING CREW

COLORING CREW

COLORING CREW

COLORING CREW

COLORING CREW

COLORING CREW

COLORING CREW

WHEN PEOPLE CALL YOU A CARROT TOP BUT THE TOPS OF CARROTS ARE FUCKING GREEN

COLORING CREW

COLORING CREW

COLORING CREW

COLORING CREW

COLORING CREW

COLORING CREW

WHEN YOU SUNBATHE AT THE BEACH BUT CUNTS KEEP STEPPING ON YOU BECAUSE YOU BLEND IN WITH THE SAND

WHEN PEOPLE DYE THEIR SHITTY HAIR RED AND START CALLING THEMSELVES A GINGER

COLORING CREW

WHEN YOUR SKIN COLOR CHOICES ARE EITHER SOUR CREAM OR FUCKING COOKED LOBSTER

COLORING CREW

COLORING CREW

COLORING CREW

COLORING CREW

COLORING CREW

COLORING CREW

COLOR TEST
PAGE

COLORING CREW

THANKS!
WE HOPE YOU HAD FUN!

IF YOU LIKED THIS BOOK THEN YOU YOU CAN
VIEW OUR FULL RANGE OF HILARIOUS ADULT
COLORING BOOKS BY GOING TO AMAZON AND
SEARCHING FOR "COLORING CREW" AND THEN
CLICKING ON OUR AUTHOR PAGE.

THANKS AGAIN!

COLORING CREW

Made in the USA
Las Vegas, NV
31 August 2021

29348259R00026